HAY FOR MY OX

A first reading-book for Waldorf Schools. Collected and arranged by Isabel Wyatt and Joan Rudel

©The Lanthorn Press 1987

Illustrations by Auvikki Mikkola

Lay-out by Arne Klingborg

ISBN 0 906155 05 3

© The Lanthorn Press 1968
Sixth Impression 1987
All Rights Reserved. No part of this publication may be reproduced or transmitted, in any form or by any means, without the prior permission of The Lanthorn Press, Peredur, East Grinstead, England.
Printed in England by Mackays of Chatham Ltd, Chatham, Kent.

CONTENTS

	page
Hay for my Ox – Isabel Wyatt	5
Brother Ox and Brother Ass – Isabel Wyatt	13
Poems: The Hare – trans. Rose Fyleman	19
Where go the Boats? – R. L. Stevenson	20
The Prince Who Kept Pigs – Isabel Wyatt	23
Mark and his Lamp – Isabel Wyatt	31
Ripe Plums in Spring – Gesta Romanorum (medieval)	38
Poems: Spring – William Blake	44
Some One – Walter de la Mare	47
The Elves' Dance – Anonymous	49
The Tree of Three Cries – Celtic Legend	51
How Sheep got Sheep-Bells – Old Legend	57
The Giant and the Child – Old Legend	63
Poems: Two Prayers – Anonymous	69
King Vincent and Lord Tom-Tit – Isabel Wyatt	71
Do Not Go into the Wood – Indian Fable	77
Poems: The Cuckoo – Anonymous	81
May Day – Anonymous	82
The Caterpillar – Christina Rossetti	84
The Rain – William H. Davies	85
The Fork-Tail and the Rams – Indian Fable	87
King Cackle – Indian Fable	89
The Monkey and the Pea – Indian Fable	95
Poems: Old Riddles – Anonymous	98

HAY FOR MY OX

An old farmer had two sons, Cross-Patch and Jeff.

Cross-Patch was a man.

But Jeff was still a boy.

Jeff had a little red ox.

This little red ox was as dear to him as if he were his son.

And so, in a way, he was.

For the old farmer had let Jeff bring up the little red ox by hand.

The old farmer died.

Cross-Patch now had the farm.

"Cross-Patch," said Jeff, "I need hay for my little red ox."

"You must need it, then," said Cross-Patch.

"You will get no hay from me."

Jeff told his little red ox:

"We must go and seek hay for you."

And off he went, to find hay for his little red ox.

His little red ox went with him.

They went a little way; they went a long way.

The way led at last to a trim little farm.

Jeff went into the farm-yard.

His little red ox went with him.

Jeff saw stalls for ten mares, and the mares in them.

He saw sheds for ten cows, and the cows in them.

He saw sties for ten hogs, and the hogs in them.

He saw a barn for ten carts, and the carts in them.

And by the wall of the barn he saw a big blue hay-cart, full of fresh, sweet hay.

It was so full that the hay spilt out.

It was the kind of hay-cart the little red ox saw in his sleep.

By it stood an old man.

He was as plump and red as a robin.

"What do you seek, farmer's boy?" he said.

"Do you seek gold? Do you seek joy?"

"No, good sir," said Jeff.

"I seek hay for my little red ox."

"If you can pass a test I will set you," said the Robin-Man, "you can have all the hay you need all the rest of your life. What do you think of that?"

"Well, and better than well, good sir," said Jeff.

The Robin-Man led Jeff to a stable.

The little red ox went with them.

The stable had big bolts and bars.

In it were five colts.

One colt had black hoofs.

One colt had white hoofs.

One colt had green hoofs.

One colt had gold hoofs.

One colt had wet hoofs.

"I will lock you in with them," said the Robin-Man.

"If you can tell me how they get such hoofs, the colts and the

trim little farm shall be yours, *and* hay for your little red ox. What do you think of that?"

"Well, and better than well, good sir," said Jeff.

He let the Robin-Man lock him in with the colts.

He lay down in the straw to sleep.

His little red ox lay down with him.

"Little Red Ox," said Jeff.

"We have four eyes, you and I.

Two eyes can shut, and two can stay open till the colts stir."

The two eyes that shut were Jeff's.

The little red ox kept his open.

Jeff slept.

But when he felt Little Red Ox butt him, up he sprang.

He saw the five colts thrust back the big bolts and bars.

He saw them rush out, with stamp of hoof, and flash of eye, and sweep of mane, and toss of tail.

He ran out, too.

And his little red ox went with him.

Jeff saw Black-Hoof swoop into the soil.

He saw Wet-Hoof swoop into the brook.

He saw Green-Hoof fly up to run on the tree-tops.

He saw White-Hoof fly up to frisk in the clouds.

He saw Gold-Hoof fly up to kick the stars.

Then all five colts were back.

They all ran to the blue hay-cart.

They all set hay on hay till it lay in banks of spilt gold.

Jeff went to find the Robin-Man.

His little red ox went with him.

Jeff told the Robin-Man:

"Black-Hoof's hoofs are black with soil.

Wet-Hoof's hoofs are wet from the brook.

Green-Hoof's hoofs are green from the tree-tops.

White-Hoof's hoofs are white from the clouds.

Gold-Hoof's hoofs are gold with star-dust.

I need all five if I am to have hay for my little red ox.

What do you think of that?"

"Well, and better than well," said the Robin-Man.

"The colts and the trim little farm are yours.

And the hay for your little red ox."

So Jeff got the colts, and the trim little farm, *and* the hay for his little red ox.

He was as glad as glad can be.

And so was his little ox with him.

BROTHER OX AND BROTHER ASS

Brother Ox and Brother Ass slept in one stable.

All day long, Brother Ox had to pull an ox-cart for Farmer, to bring in his corn and hay.

Tim was Farmer's small son.

Brother Ass was Tim's pet.

So Brother Ass had no farm-tasks to do.

He had all day to kick up his heels in the sun.

Tim was born under a lucky star.

If you are born under that lucky star, you can tell what a dog or a cat or an ox or an ass says.

But it has to be when that lucky star is in the sky.

Tim saw his lucky star in the sky when he went to bed.

He stood to look at it.

The stable had a roof of reeds.

The wind had torn a gap in this roof.

Tim saw that this gap was lit up.

So out to the stable Tim went on the tips of his toes.

Farmer had left a ladder by the stable wall, to mend the gap in the roof next day.

Up the ladder, as fast as an adder, went Tim, to look in at the gap in the roof.

He saw that Farmer had left his stable-lamp hung on the wall, still lit.

He saw Brother Ox and Brother Ass, each in his stall.

"Brother Ass," said Brother Ox, "how lucky you are!

You have no farm-tasks to do.

You have all day to kick up your heels in the sun.

But all day *I* have to pull an ox-cart, full of corn and hay."

"Brother Ox," said Brother Ass, "why do you do it?

When they try to put you in the shafts, do not let them.

You must tramp, and stamp, and butt, and toss, and rip up the grass.

Then you, too, need do no farm-tasks.

You, too, can have all day to kick up your heels in the sun."

"I will try it, Brother Ass," said Brother Ox.

Next day, Farmer said to Tim:

"Tim, keep away from Brother Ox.

When I went to put him in the shafts, he went mad."

"Brother Ass told him to do that," said Tim.

And he told Farmer all that Brother Ox and Brother Ass had said.

"Well, well, well!" said Farmer.

"What prank will Brother Ass get up to next?"

Farmer went to the stable.

He put Brother Ass in the shafts of the ox-cart.

All day Brother Ass had to pull it, full of corn and hay.

All day Brother Ox was free to kick up his heels in the sun.

As soon as Tim's lucky star lit up the sky, Tim went out to the stable on the tips of his toes.

Up the ladder, as fast as an adder, he went, to look in at the gap in the roof.

"Brother Ass," said Brother Ox, "I did just as you told me. And what a day I have had!

All day I have been free to kick up my heels in the sun."

"Brother Ox," said Brother Ass, "I bring you such bad news. Farmer says that if you are too mad to pull the ox-cart, he may as well kill you."

"No! Did he?" cried Brother Ox.

"I must pull it, then.

For I do not wish to die just yet."

So, next day, when Farmer went to put him in the cart-shafts, Brother Ox was meek and mild.

"Tim," said Farmer, "we must find a farm-task for Brother Ass to do.

If we do not, he will find new pranks to play on us."

"Let me go to the mill with the corn for Miller to grind," said Tim.

"I can put the corn in two bags, and sling them on the back

of Brother Ass.

And that can be his farm-task."

"Yes, do that," said Farmer.

So Tim did.

"I wish I had not told Brother Ox to go mad," said Brother Ass.

"I never seem free now to kick up my heels in the sun!"

THE HARE

Between the valley and the hill
    There sat a little hare;
It nibbled at the grass until
    The ground was nearly bare.

And when the ground was nearly bare
    It rested in the sun;
A hunter came and saw it there
    And shot it with his gun.

It thought it must be dead, be dead,
    But, wonderful to say,
It found it was alive instead
    And quickly ran away.

                German nursery-rhyme translated by
                          Rose Fyleman.

WHERE GO THE BOATS?

Dark brown is the river,
Golden is the sand.
It flows along for ever,
With trees on either hand.

Green leaves a-floating,
Castles of the foam,
Boats of mine a-boating –
Where will all come home?

On goes the river
And out past the mill,
Away down the valley,
Away down the hill.

Away down the river,
A hundred miles or more,
Other little children
Shall bring my boats ashore.
                R. L. Stevenson.

THE PRINCE WHO KEPT PIGS

Prince Harry was the son of a king. When Prince Harry was still a boy, the king died. His foe won the land.

The new king sent Prince Harry to Hog Rock. On Hog Rock an old swine-herd kept the king's pigs. Prince Harry had to help him.

On each side of Hog Rock it was sea all the way to the sky. But one clear day, Prince Harry saw cliffs a long way off.

He said to the old swine-herd:

"What land is that?"

And the old swine-herd told him:

"It is a land *not* to try to get to. In that land all men go in fear of a mad wild boar."

Prince Harry said to his pigs:

"I *will* try to get to that land, mad boar or no mad boar. For if I can do that, I shall be free."

But how was he to get to that land? It was far too far to swim. And he had no boat to float in. And he had no tools.

The old swine-herd kept the sows and the small pigs in sties near his hut. Each day he sent Prince Harry out into the wood with the big hogs that had to get fat.

All day long, the hogs fed on the nuts that fell from the trees. When they saw Prince Harry pick up a stick, they ran to him with grunts of joy. They stood still, for him to scratch them with his stick on the back and ears. Then they lay and slept.

In this way seven years went by. Prince Harry was now a man.

Then, one day, the sea cast up a log on the sands.

The old swine-herd slept each noon. So now, each noon, Prince Harry left his hogs to feed in the woods. He ran down to the log on the sands.

He took sharp flints. With them, bit by bit, he dug a boat out of the log. He had a branch for a mast. He had two sticks for oars.

But he still had to stay on Hog Rock till a west wind blew.

Day after day after day, the wind blew all ways but that way.

At last, one day, a brisk west wind sprang up.

Prince Harry left his hogs to feed in the wood. Down to the sands he ran.

Push, pull; push, pull; push, pull – *splash,* and his boat was afloat on the sea.

He hung his coat on the mast, to catch that brisk west wind.

He took an oar in each hand. And over the sea he sped.

Rock, roll; rock, roll; rock, roll; tip, toss; tip, toss; tip, toss. On he went, with the help of that brisk west wind.

Hog Rock was soon a dot in the sea at his back. The cliffs in front of him grew clear. The cliffs in front of him grew near. Now he saw the walls of a town on the cliff. Now he saw a wood. Then the sea fell on him.

It flung him up. It flung him down. It flung him on the sands at the foot of the cliff.

Men saw him from the walls of the town. They ran down the

cliff-path to him.

They held him up by the heels, to pour the sea out of him.

They put him flat on the sands, to pump and thump the sea out of him.

Soon Prince Harry sat up.

He said to the men:

"Do you still go in fear of a mad wild boar in this land?"

"We do," they said.

"Then bring me to your king," said Prince Harry.

"We have no king," they told him. "Our king has just died. His only child is now our queen. She will marry the man who kills the mad wild boar."

"Then bring me a sack and a spear," said Prince Harry.

He took the sack and the spear. He went up the cliff. He went into the wood.

In the wood, he went from tree to tree, to pick nuts, till his sack was full.

The mad wild boar smelt the smell of man in the wood, His

eyes went red. Froth fell from his lips.

After that smell of man shot the mad wild boar – dash, clash, crash, splash, smash. Prince Harry fled up a tree. The mad wild boar sped at the tree.

His tusks were long. His tusks were strong. At each rush of that mad wild boar, Prince Harry felt the tree rock. At each rush of that mad wild boar, Prince Harry felt the twigs thrash. He flung down nuts from his sack. As soon as the wild boar saw the nuts, he stood and fed on them. Prince Harry flung down more nuts, and still more nuts, till he had flung down all he had.

At last the wild boar was full-fed. Then Prince Harry held fast to the tree with his legs and his left hand. He bent from his branch, to scratch the back and the ears of the mad wild boar with the tip of his spear.

Grunt, grunt, grunt, went the mad wild boar in joy. He stood still for the tip of the spear to scratch him. And at last he lay down and slept.

Then deep into the wild boar's neck Prince Harry thrust his spear. And that was the end of the fear that lay on that land. Prince Harry went back to the town on the cliff. He sent men to drag the wild boar in, for all to see.

The queen ran out of the town to meet Prince Harry. She drew him in with both hands.

"It is *your* town, and *your* land, now," she told him. "From this day you are its king. But tell me how you did it? When other men went to kill him, the mad wild boar rent them to bits."

"They did not know all *I* know," said Prince Harry. "They had not kept pigs for seven years!"

MARK AND HIS LAMP

A king had ten sons. The last son was still a boy. This was
Prince Mark. The king died. He left his land to his ten sons.
But the nine sons who were men said:
"Why must we let Mark have a part of the land? He is still a
boy. Let us send him to look for luck in far-off lands."
So they put a big hat on his head, to keep off the sun.
They put a big bag on his back, full of crusts for the way.
In his hand they put a big staff, with a steel tip to it.
On his feet they put big rag boots.
And they sent him to look for luck in far-off lands.
Mark set off. He went on and on till four ways met.
He did not know the way to go. So he sat with his back to a
tree, and a crust from his bag in his hand.
A little old man went by. He was bent in two. A lamp hung

and swung from his hand.

"I wish *I* had a crust," said the little old man.

"Have one, you dear little old man," said Mark.

And he put a crust from his bag in the old man's hand.

The little old man sat by Mark, with *his* back to a tree, and a crust in *his* hand.

Munch, crunch, went the little old man.

Munch, crunch, went Mark.

"How old are you, you dear little old man?" said Mark.

"Not so old as all that," said the little old man. "Only five hundred years."

"Then, you dear little old man," said Mark, "can you tell me the best land to look for luck in?"

And the little old man told him:

"You must go as far as the wind can blow. You must go as far as the rain can wet. You must go as far as the sea can flow. You must go as far as the sun can run."

"And how shall I tell when I get as far as that, you dear little old man?" said Mark.

"This lamp will tell you," said the little old man. "This lamp will go out when you get to the end of your way. Then you must put down roots, and grow."

"Can you show me the way, you dear little old man?" said Mark.

"Hold up the lamp," said the little old man.

Mark held up the lamp. It lit up the way to the left.

"That is the way to the land you seek," said the little old man. "And that is the way you must go."

So that was the way Mark went. He went by day; he went by dark. Not a wink of sleep, not a blink of sleep, did he get. The little old man's lamp lit up his way.

"Jog on, jog on," sang Mark. "I must go as far as the wind can blow. I must go as far as the rain can wet. I must go as far as the sea can flow. I must go as far as the sun can run."

On and on he went, till his big bag had no crusts left in it.

On and on he went, till the steel tip of his staff was worn down to the wood.

On and on he went, till his big hat hung from his head in wisps.

On and on he went, till his big rag boots hung from his feet in shreds.

And still the little old man's lamp lit up his way.

He went as far as the wind can blow. He went as far as the rain can wet. He went as far as the sea can flow. He went as far as the sun can run.

And then his lamp went out.

Mark went to the king of that land. The king of that land was little and old.

"I think I must be at the end of my way, you dear little old king," said Mark.

"I need a boy who is at the end of his way," said the little old king. "But he must be the son of a king."

"That is just what I am, you dear little old king," said Mark. He did not look the son of a king, with his worn staff in his hand, and the bag on his back, and his big hat that hung in

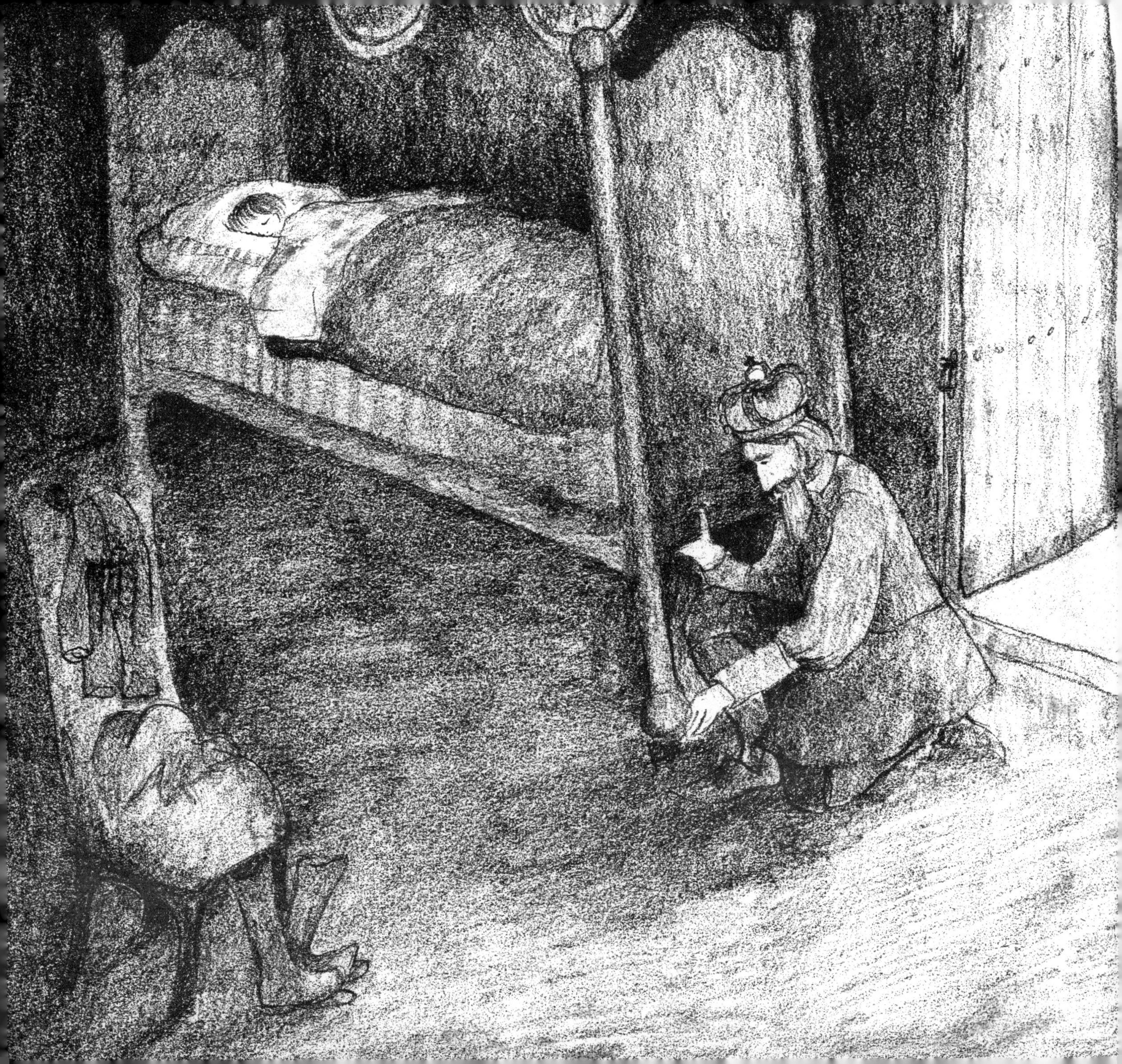

wisps, and his big rag boots that hung in shreds.

"I will tell you if you *are* the son of a king when you have slept," said the little old king.

So Mark went off to bed. As soon as he put down his head, he slept and he slept and he slept.

Then in went the little old king on tip-toe. Under each of Mark's four bed-posts he slid an ivy-leaf. Then out on tip-toe went the little old king. And still Mark slept and slept and slept.

"Did you sleep well?" said the little old king, next day.

"So well, you dear little old king," said Mark, "that I did not feel you put me in a fresh bed."

"But I did not put you in a fresh bed," said the little old king. "Why do you think I did?"

"I will tell you, you dear little old king," said Mark. "When I sat up to rub the sleep from my eyes, the bed felt less low than the bed I went to sleep in."

"How much less low?" said the little old king.

"Oh, a lot, you dear little old king," said Mark. "As much as a flat ivy-leaf."

Then said the little old king:

"That tells me that you *are* the son of a king. And *I* will tell *you* why I need one. I have no son. I need a king's son, to bring up as *my* son, to be king of this land when I die. Are you willing?"

"Willing and more than willing, you dear little old king," said Mark.

Then he knew that this *was* the end of his way. And he did as the little old man had told him – he put down roots, and grew.

RIPE PLUMS IN SPRING

Bob was as strong as an ox.

But Bob was as poor as a wren.

"One day I will ask the king to let me be his man," said Bob. "Kings have need of strong men. But how can I get to see the king, clad in rags as I am?"

Bob went into the wood one day in Spring. The trees were full of green buds. But one tree was full of ripe plums.

"Ripe plums in Spring?" cried Bob. "I never saw such a thing till now! I will pick them for the king. In this way I can get to see him, and he may let me be his man."

So Bob took off his hood, to put the ripe plums in. When the hood was full, he put green weeds on top. The green weeds kept the ripe plums fresh.

Then Bob set off with his hood of ripe plums, to go to the king.

He went to the king's gate. At the king's gate sat the king's porter. The king's porter saw Bob's rags.

"Be off with you, beggar!" cried the king's porter. "Or I will cuff your ears till you see stars!"

"Good sir, let me in," said Bob. "I bring a gift for the king."

The porter took up the green weeds from the top of the hood. He saw it was full of ripe plums.

"Ripe plums in Spring?" cried the porter. "I never saw such a thing till now! The king will pay you well for such a gift. I will let you in. But I must have a third of what you get for them."

"You shall have it," said Bob.

So the king's porter let Bob in at the king's gate. And Bob went on to the door of the king's hall.

At the door of the king's hall sat the king's door-keeper. The king's door-keeper saw Bob's rags.

"Be off with you, beggar!" cried the king's door-keeper. "Or you will feel your ribs rattle!"

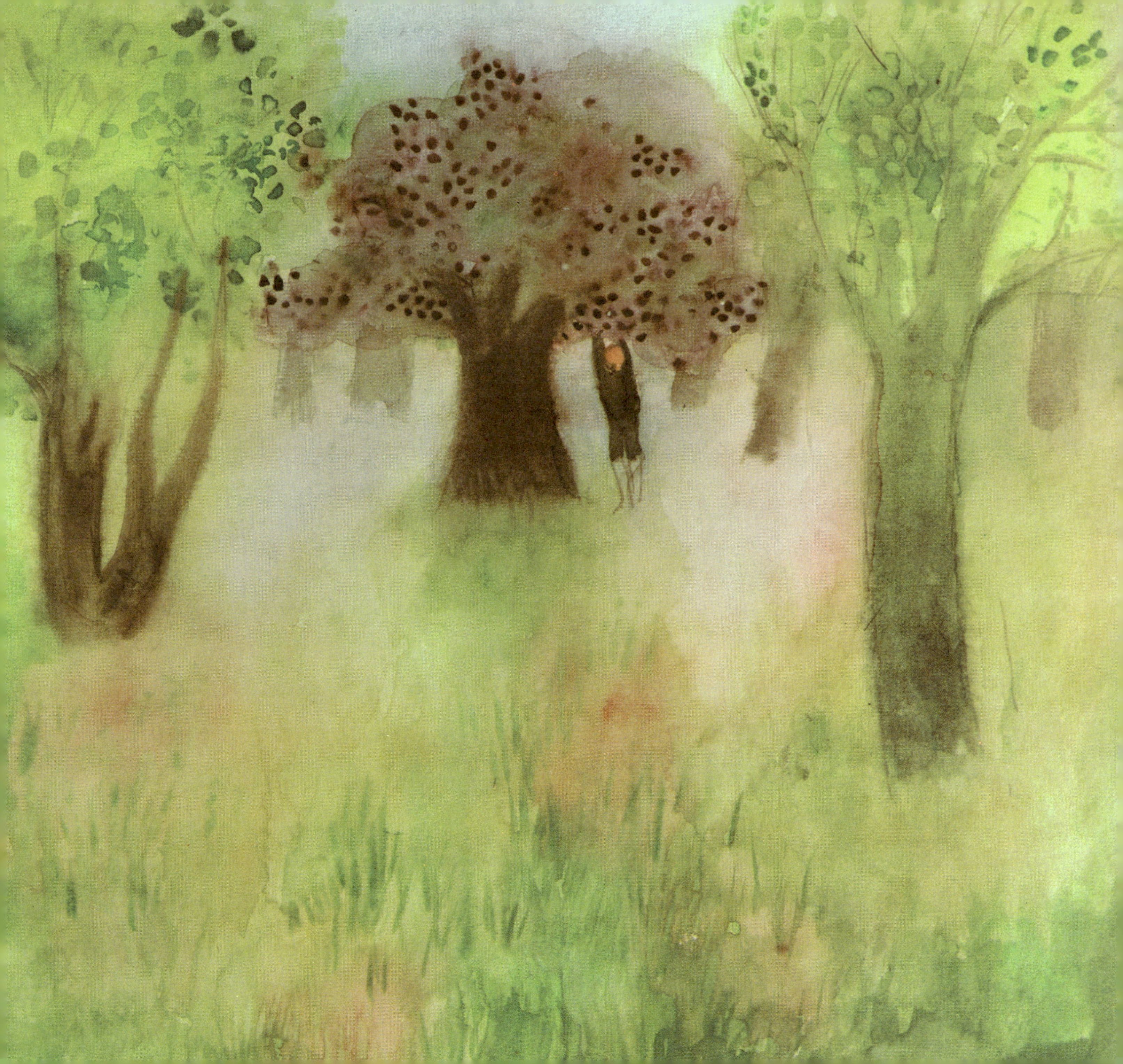

"Good sir, let me in," said Bob. "I bring a gift for the king."

The door-keeper took up the green weeds from the top of the hood. He saw it was full of ripe plums.

"Ripe plums in Spring?" cried the door-keeper. "I never saw such a thing till now! The king will pay you well for such a gift. I will let you in. But I must have a third of what you get for them."

"You shall have it," said Bob.

So the king's door-keeper let Bob into the king's hall. And Bob went on to the door of the king's room.

At the door of the king's room sat the king's groom. The king's groom saw Bob's rags.

"Be off with you, beggar!" cried the king's groom. "Or I will sweep you off your legs!"

"Good sir, let me in," said Bob. "I bring a gift for the king."

The groom took up the green weeds from the top of the hood. He saw it was full of ripe plums.

"Ripe plums in Spring?" cried the groom. "I never saw such

a thing till now! The king will pay you well for such a gift. I will let you in. But I must have a third of what you get for them."

"You shall have it," said Bob.

So the king's groom let Bob into the king's room. Bob went to the king. He bent to his feet.

"Lord King," said Bob, "I bring you this gift."

The king took up the green weeds from the top of the hood. He saw it was full of ripe plums.

"Ripe plums in Spring?" cried the king. "I never saw such a thing till now! It is the best of gifts. What gift will *you* have from *me*?"

"Lord King, three blows, to give as I wish," said Bob.

"They are yours," said the king.

"Then, Lord King," said Bob, "send for your groom, your door-keeper and your porter."

The king sent for them. They stood in front of him.

Bob went to the king's porter.

"Good sir," he said, "I give you your third of what I got for my plums."

Whish-swish went Bob's fist. That porter got such a cuff on the ear that he saw stars.

Bob went to the king's door-keeper.

"Good sir," he said, "I give you your third of what I got for my plums."

Whish-swish went Bob's fist. That door-keeper got such a cuff that he felt his ribs rattle.

Bob went to the king's groom.

"Good sir," he said, "I give you your third of what I got for my plums."

Whish-swish went Bob's fist. That groom got such a cuff that it swept him off his legs.

"Bless us!" cried the king. "The man is as strong as an ox! Good man, will you be *my* man? Kings have need of such strong men as you."

And so Bob got his wish.

SPRING

Sound the Flute!
Now it's mute.
Birds delight
Day and Night
Nightingale
In the dale,
Lark in Sky,
Merrily
Merrily, Merrily, to welcome in the Year.

Little Boy,
Full of Joy;
Little Girl,
Sweet and Small;
Cock does crow,
So do you;
Merry voice,
Infant noise,
Merrily, Merrily, to welcome in the Year.

Little Lamb,
Here I am;
Come and lick
My white neck;
Let me pull
Your soft Wool;
Let me Kiss
Your soft face:
Merrily, Merrily, to welcome in the Year.

WILLIAM BLAKE

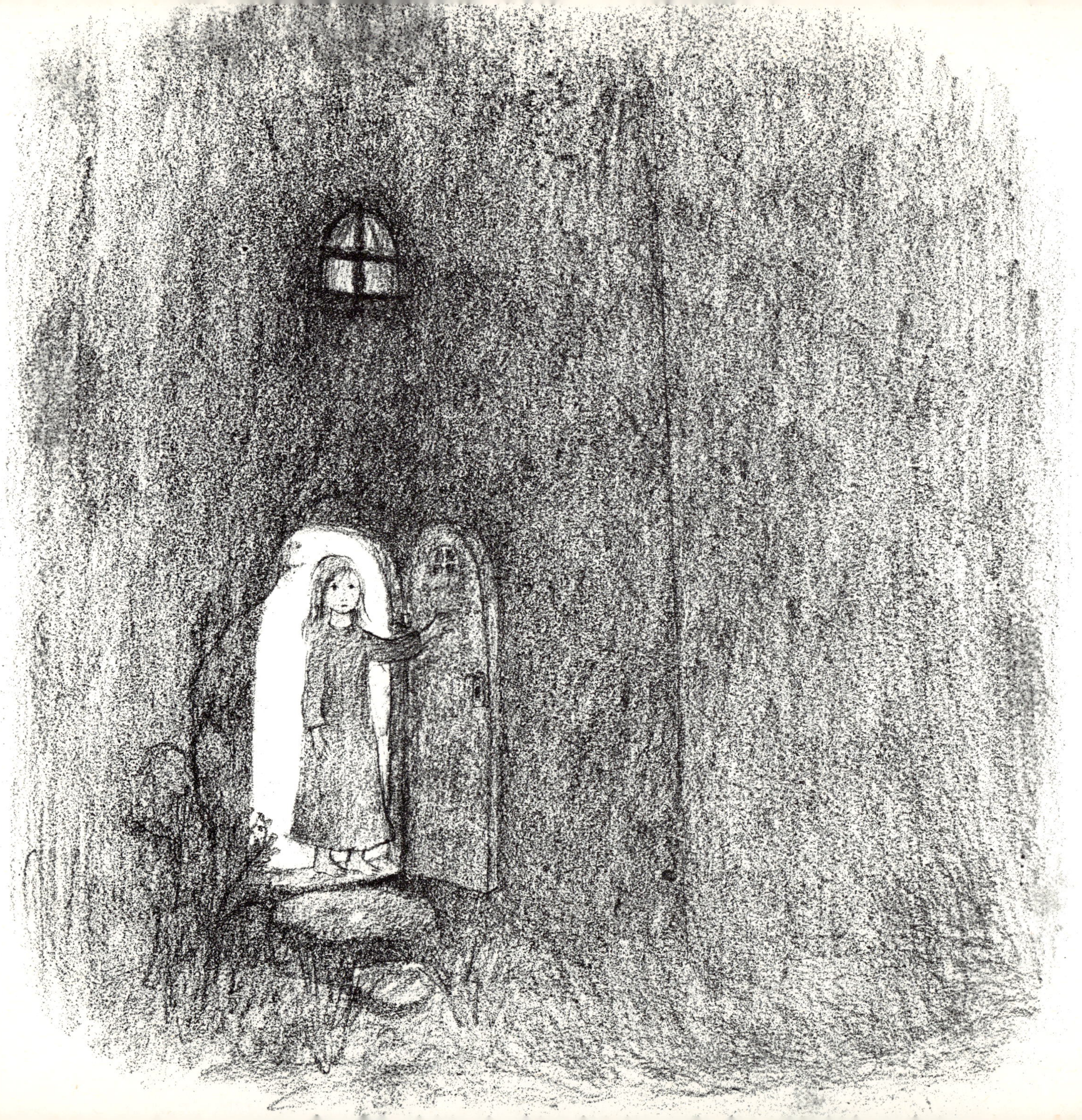

SOME ONE

Some one came knocking
At my wee, small door;
Some one came knocking
I'm sure – sure – sure;
I listened, I opened,
I looked from left to right,
But nought there was a-stirring
In the still dark night;

Only the busy beetle
Tap-tapping in the wall,
Only from the forest
The screeching owl call,

Only the cricket whistling
While the dew drops fall,
So I know not who came knocking,
At all, At all, At all.
     WALTER DE LA MARE

THE ELVES' DANCE

Round about, round about
In a fair ring-a,
Thus we dance, thus we dance
And thus we sing-a,
Trip and go, to and fro
Over this green-a,
All about, in and out,
For our brave Queen-a.

ANONYMOUS

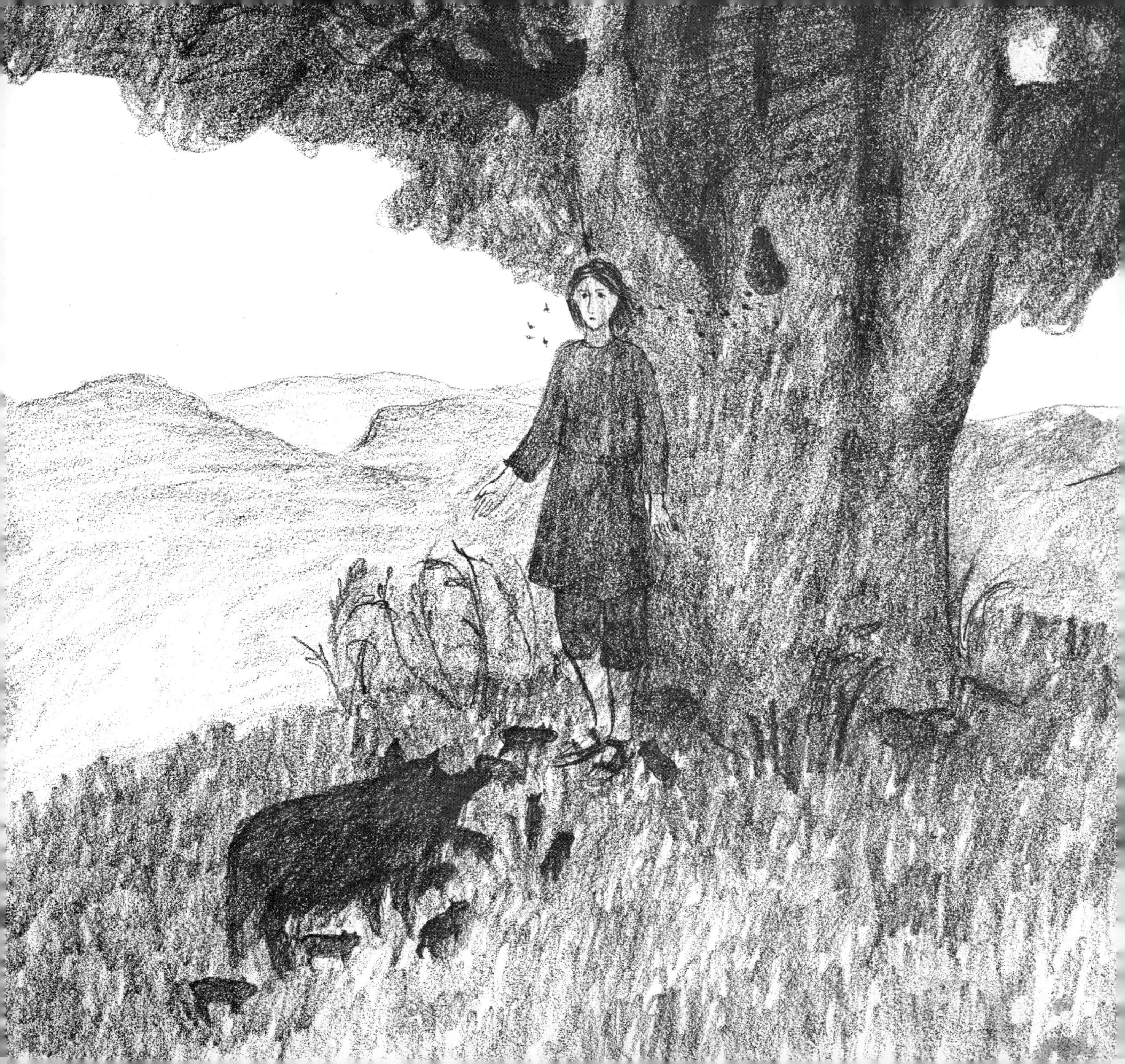

THE TREE OF THREE CRIES

An old monk had his hut in the wild Welsh land, to teach its wild Welsh men. Baglan was a boy he had with him, to help him.

When Baglan grew up, the old monk said to him:

"Baglan, you must do as I do. You must go to a fresh spot in this wild Welsh land. You, too, must teach its wild Welsh men."

"How can I tell the way to go?" said Baglan.

"A baglan shall tell you," said the old monk.

And he put a crook in Baglan's hand. For in Welsh, *baglan* is a crook.

And the old monk told him:

"At each cross-way, you must stand the crook up. And the way the crook falls, go that way. That will be the way to the spot you seek; and that is the way you must go."

"How can I tell when I reach the spot I seek?" said Baglan next.

And the old monk told him:

"When you reach a tree of three cries, that is the spot you seek."

So Baglan set out with his crook.

On three legs he went. At each cross-way he stood the crook up; and the way the crook fell, that was the way he went.

"That is the way to the spot I seek," he said. "And that is the way I must go."

His crook led him at last to the top of a big hill. A big tree stood at the top of this hill.

At the foot of the tree lay a wild sow, with ten little pigs. At the top of the tree was a rooks' nest. Wild bees swept in and out of a gap in the trunk of the tree.

As Baglan went to the tree, the sow and her ten little pigs ran to meet him, and to greet him with a *grunt, grunt, grunt.*

The rooks flew on big black wings to meet him, and to greet

him with a *caw, caw, caw.*

The wild bees swept to meet him, and to greet him with a *buzz, buzz, buzz.*

Baglan stood his crook at the foot of the tree. It did not fall this way or that way. It just stood.

"This must be the tree of three cries," said Baglan. "This is the spot I seek; and this is the spot I must stay in."

Baglan did not think the top of a big hill a good spot to put up his hut on. So to put up his hut he went to the foot of the hill.

Each day, he put up a bit of his hut. But the bit he put up each day just fell, *smash,* as soon as he slept.

So back he went to the top of the hill.

The pigs, big and little, dug up rocks at the foot of the tree for him, with a *grunt, grunt, grunt* of joy.

The rooks flew off each day, to bring back crusts for him, with a *caw, caw, caw* of joy.

The bees swept out from the tree-trunk each day with bits of sweet honey-comb for him, with a *buzz, buzz, buzz* of joy.

"How blest am I," said Baglan, "in this tree of three cries!"

So Baglan put up his hut at the foot of the tree.

He left a gap at the foot of the wall of the hut. This was for the wild sow and her ten little pigs to go in and out by.

He left a gap six feet up the wall of the hut. This was for the wild bees to go in to the tree-trunk by.

He left a gap in the roof, by the top of the tree. This was for the rooks to go in to the rooks' nest by.

A wild Welsh man of that wild Welsh land saw Baglan's hut. He went back and told what he had seen. The wild Welsh men went to see Baglan, three of them, six of them, ten of them, twenty of them, fifty of them.

Baglan sat by his hut to teach them.

Under the tree of the three cries, the wild Welsh men sat still, for Baglan to teach them.

The wild pigs lay still at his feet, for Baglan to teach them, too.

The wild bees hung still in the tree-trunk, for Baglan to teach them, too.

The rooks sat still in the tree-top, for Baglan to teach them, too. At this tree of the three cries, wild rooks and wild bees and wild pigs and wild Welsh men met day by day, for Baglan to bless them.

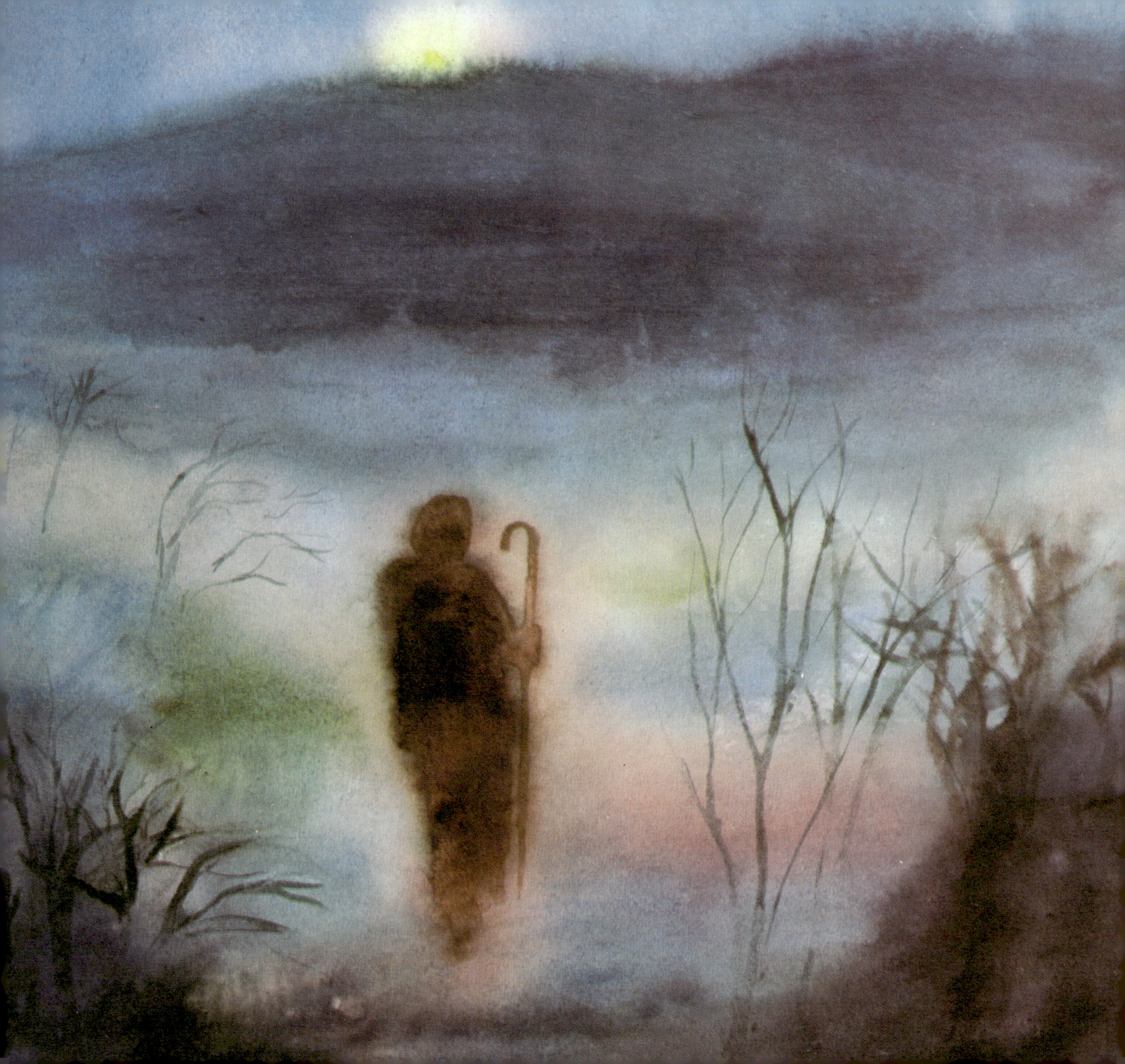

HOW SHEEP GOT SHEEP-BELLS

All day the sheep went up on the hills, to crop the sweet hill-grass and get fat. At dusk, Otto the Shepherd went up with his crook, to bring them all back to the sheep-fold.

The sheep went into the sheep-fold. But Black-Sheep was not with them. So Otto the Shepherd took his crook, and back he went to find her.

The mist was thick now on the hills. To and fro, to and fro in the mist went Otto the Shepherd, till he had lost his way. Then – one step, and he was out of the mist. Two steps, and his feet were on a sheep-track. Three steps, and with a cry of joy he saw a star glow low in the sky.

"But *is* it a star?" said Otto the Shepherd. "Or is it a lamp on the hill-top?"

The sheep-track led him up and up, to a cleft in the rock on the hill-top. The star was a glow in a gap in that steep wall of rock.

Out of that gap blew a cry:

"Baa-aa-aa!"

Otto the Shepherd bent to look in.

He saw a vast cave, lit by the glow of gold. In it, clad all in gold, a king lay deep in sleep. His men, clad in gold and steel, lay with him, rank on rank.

By them stood Black-Sheep.

"Black-Sheep!" Otto the Shepherd cried to her.

"Baa-aa-aa!" she cried back.

And with a jump of joy she ran to him.

It was a steep spring for Black-Sheep up to the gap. Otto the Shepherd held out his crook, to help her up. It struck a big bell of gold that hung over the gap.

Clink, clang, Clink, clang, the bell rang out, with a clash of gold on gold. The cave shook with its clash. Otto the Shepherd felt the hill rock.

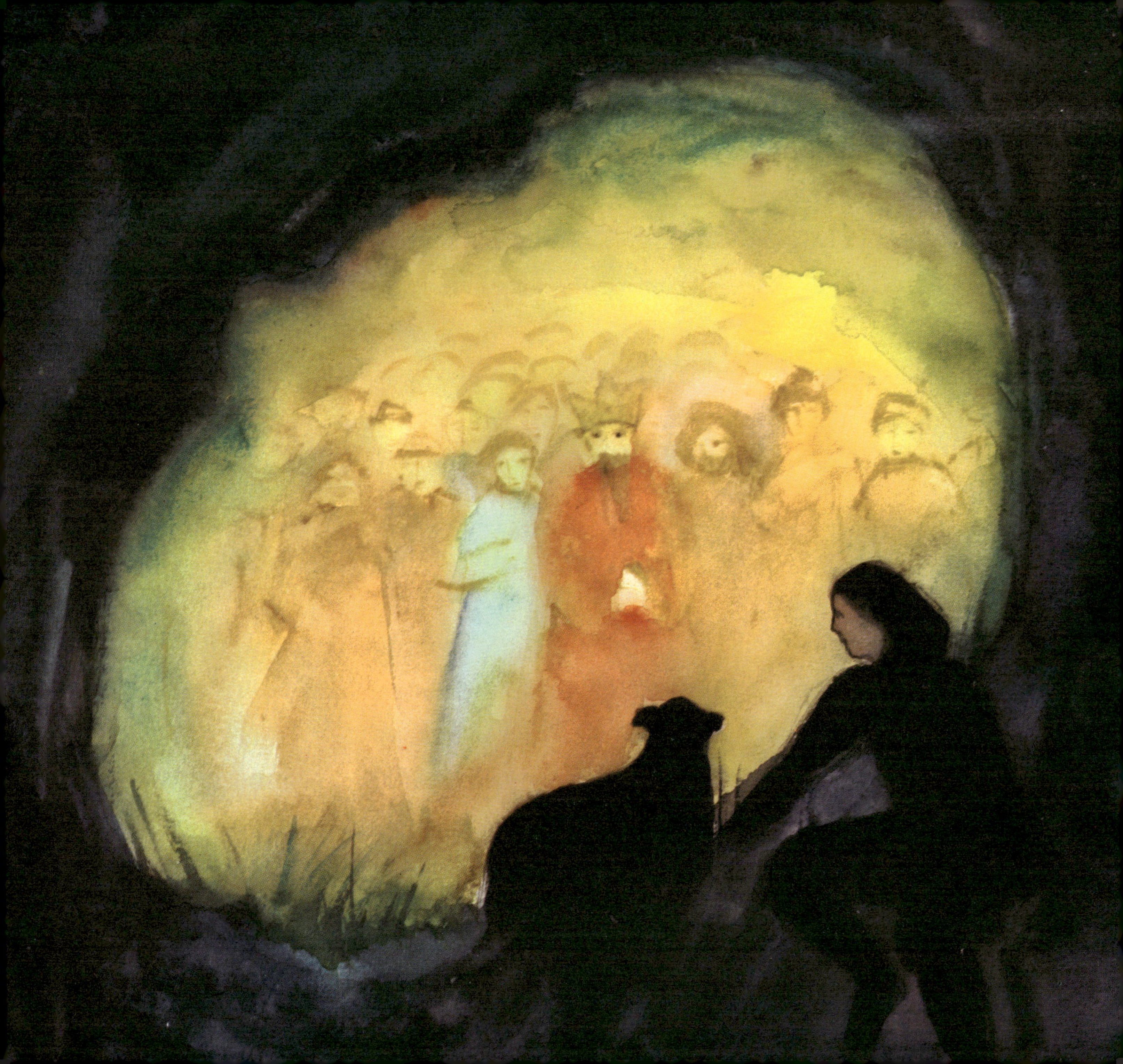

In the cave, the gold-clad king sprang to his feet. All his men sprang up with him. The cave rang with the clash of gold on gold. The cave rang with the clang of steel on steel.

"Who rang the bell?" cried the king. "Is the land in need of my help?"

Otto the Shepherd cried back:

"Not yet! Not yet! Sleep on! Sleep on! Sleep on!"

"Sleep on! Sleep on!" said the king to his men. "The land is not in need of us yet."

The king sank back to sleep. All his men sank back to sleep with him.

"So that is a bell, is it?" said Otto the Shepherd to Black-Sheep. He bent in the gap, to get a good look. For he had not seen a bell till then. His land had no bells in his day.

"Black-Sheep," he said, "if I hang such a bell from your neck, it will help me to find you when next you get lost. What do you say to that?"

"Baa-aa-aa!" said Black-Sheep.

Otto the Shepherd went from the hill-top. Black-Sheep went with him. By now the moon was up. It lit the sheep-track that led them back to the sheep-fold.

Next day, Otto the Shepherd saw that Black-Sheep's wool was thick with gold-dust. A tuft of that wool sold now and then met all his needs.

He took a tuft to the black-smith.

"This is to pay for a bell to hang from Black-Sheep's neck," Otto the Shepherd told him.

"A bell?" said the black-smith. "What is a bell?"

Otto the Shepherd told him.

Otto the Shepherd got his bell. He hung it from Black-Sheep's neck. *Chink-chink, clink-clink* went the bell when the sheep went up on the hills to get fat. *Chink-chink, clink-clink* went the bell, and led Otto the Shepherd to Black-Sheep when she got lost. And that was how sheep got sheep-bells.

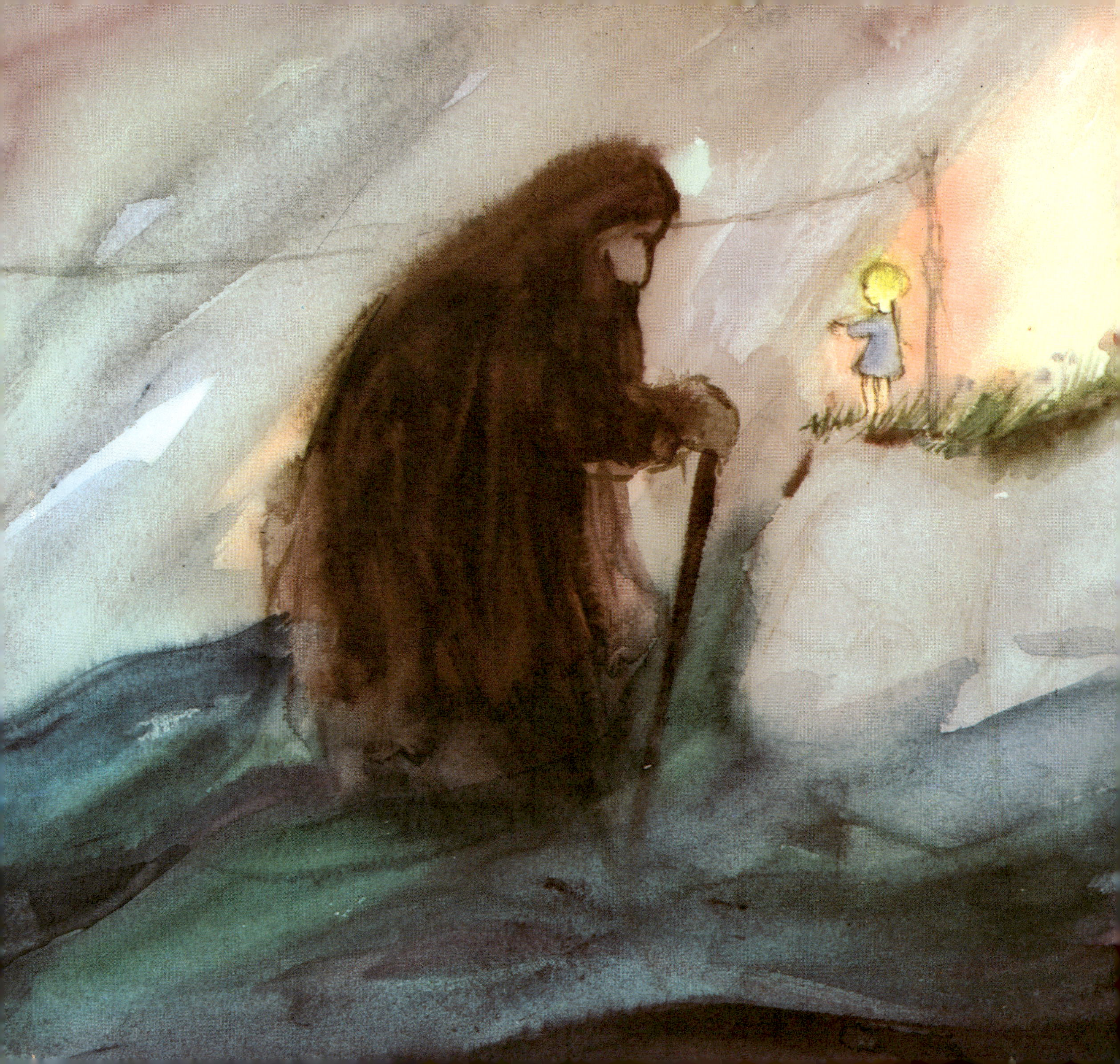

THE GIANT AND THE CHILD

Long, long ago, a giant was as bad as he was big. He was as big as six men; he was as bad as ten.

He was as strong as ten men, too.

He told a bold monk so, one day. But the bold monk did not bat an eye-lash.

The bold monk said:

"It is good to be strong, if we help men with this gift. The King who is *my* king did; and no-one is as strong as he."

"If I am less strong than he is," said the giant, "he is fit to be *my* king, and I, too, will help men. How can I do this?"

The bold monk told him:

"You can bear men over the river on your back. For it is too big and too deep and too fast for them to cross."

And when shall I see my so strong king?" said the giant.

"When you do not think to see him," said the monk.

"Then who will tell me who he is?" said the giant.

"You will not need to be told," said the monk.

"Shall *I* tell *him* who I am?" said the giant.

"*He* will tell *you*," said the monk.

The giant cut the twigs from a tree; and he took the trunk for a staff, to help him over the river.

He went to the bank of the river. On its brink he put tree-trunk on tree-trunk till he had a hut to rest in.

He slung a big bell on the wall of the hut, for men to call him with. From it he hung a long string for them to pull, to ring the bell.

When men rang the bell, *ding-dong, ding-dong,* he went to them. He bent his long legs; he bent his long back; he swung them up on his back.

And in seven giant steps he took them over the river.

One winter day it was cold as cold and wet as wet. The wind was wild. The river went by with a rush. It flung up spray at the giant's hut.

"No-one will wish to cross on such a wild day," said the giant. "I can stay snug in bed, and get a good long sleep."

He had just got snug in his bed when the big bell rang. It did not ring *ding-dong, ding-dong;* it rang a small, small *ting-a-ling-a-ling*.

Up the giant got from his bed. He took his big, strong staff in his big, strong hand. And out into the cold, wet wind he went.

And who stood by the bell-string?

Who but a small, small child!

The wind swung that small, small child. The spray stung that small, small child. But that small, small child just clung to the bell-string; and he stood as still as still.

"Can you bear me over the river, good Giant?" said the small, small child.

"On my hand," said the giant.

"On your back will be best, good Giant," said the small, small child. "I may not be as small as you think."

The giant swung the small, small child up on his back. And into the river, the deep, cold, fast, wild river, the giant went. He took one giant step in the river. It felt as if he had no-one on his back.

"What a small, small child," said the giant, "is this small, small child!"

He took two giant steps in the river. Now he felt the child big on his back.

"This small, small child," said the giant, "must be a man!"

He took three giant steps in the river. Now he bent under the child on his back.

"This small, small child," said the giant, "must be a tree!"

He took four giant steps in the river. The child on his back bent him till he clung to his staff.

"This small, small child," said the giant, "must be a hill!"

He took five giant steps in the river. The child was now so big that the giant sank to his hips.

"This small, small child," said the giant, "must be the sky!"

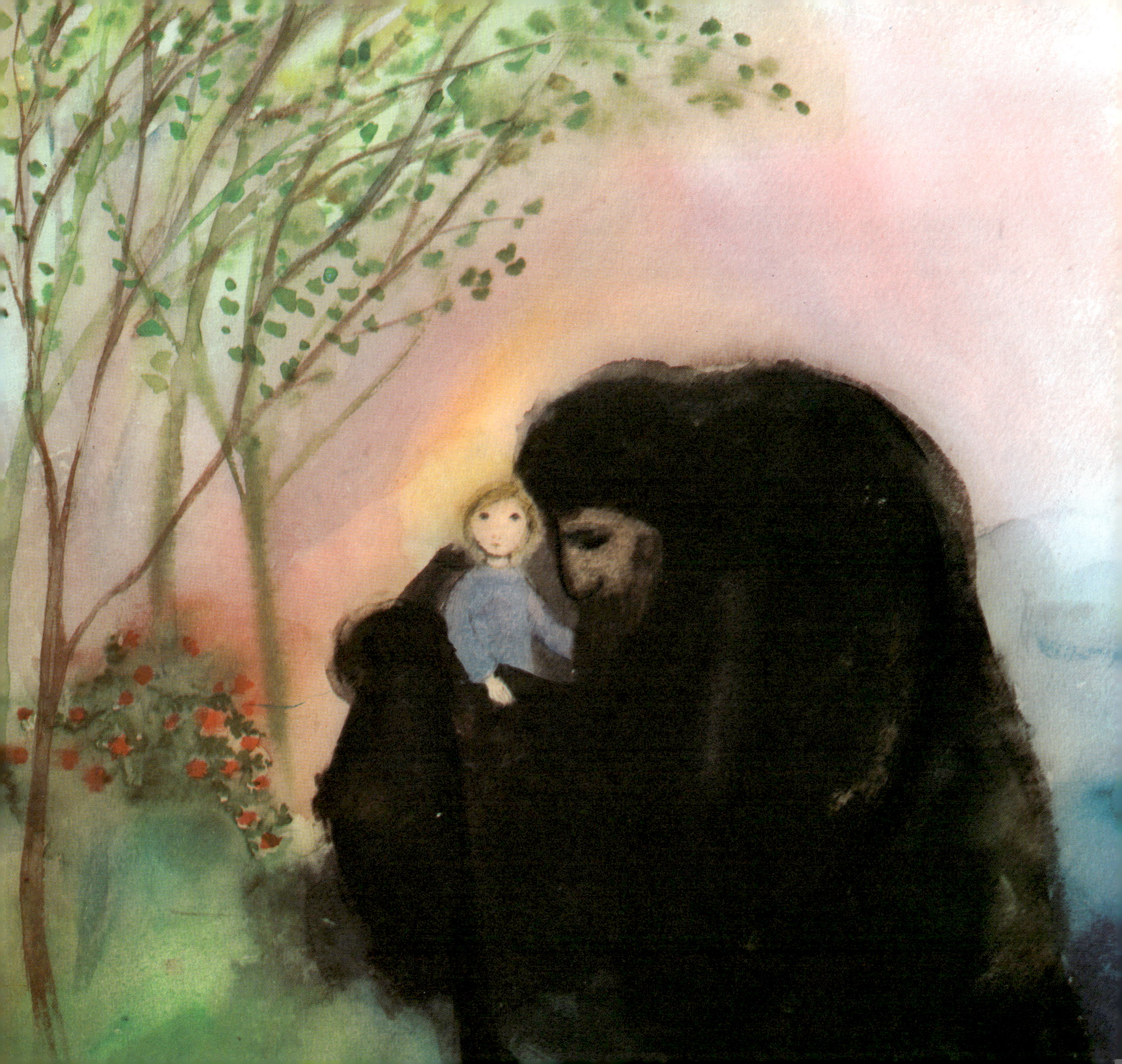

He took six giant steps in the river. The child on his back lit all the land.

"This small, small child," said the giant, "must be the sun!"

He took seven giant steps in the river. He bent his long legs; he bent his long back; he bent his long neck; and he set the small, small child dry-shod on the bank.

On the bank the winter grass was as fresh as if it were spring. The winter trees were as full of buds as if it were spring.

"This small, small child," said the giant, "must be my king!"

"Yes, I am your king, good Giant," said the small, small child. "And from now on, *you* are Christopher, He-who-bears-the-Christ."

And from then on, the giant *was* Christopher.

TWO PRAYERS OF OLDEN DAYS

God be in my head
And in my understanding,
God be in mine eyes
And in my looking,
God be in my mouth
And in my speaking,
God be in my heart
And in my thinking,
God be at mine end
And at my departing.

Matthew, Mark, Luke and John,

Bless the bed that I lie on,

Four corners to my bed,

Four angels round my head;

One to watch and one to pray

And two to bear my soul away.

                                        ANONYMOUS

KING VINCENT AND LORD TOM-TIT

Lord Tom-Tit was a small brown bird, just one inch tall. He and Lady Tom-Tit fed in King Vincent's rye-patch.

But they did not feed *on* King Vincent's rye. They kept it free from green-fly.

To and fro they swung on the weeds at the side of King Vincent's rye-patch. *Peck,* they went at the seeds of the weeds, as they clung to them up-side-down.

One day, King Vincent went to look at his rye-patch. He saw the tall weeds at the side of it.

He said to his men:

"How long have weeds stood at the side of my rye-patch?"

"So long, O King," said his men, "that no-one can say *how* long."

"Then get them all up by next week," said King Vincent.

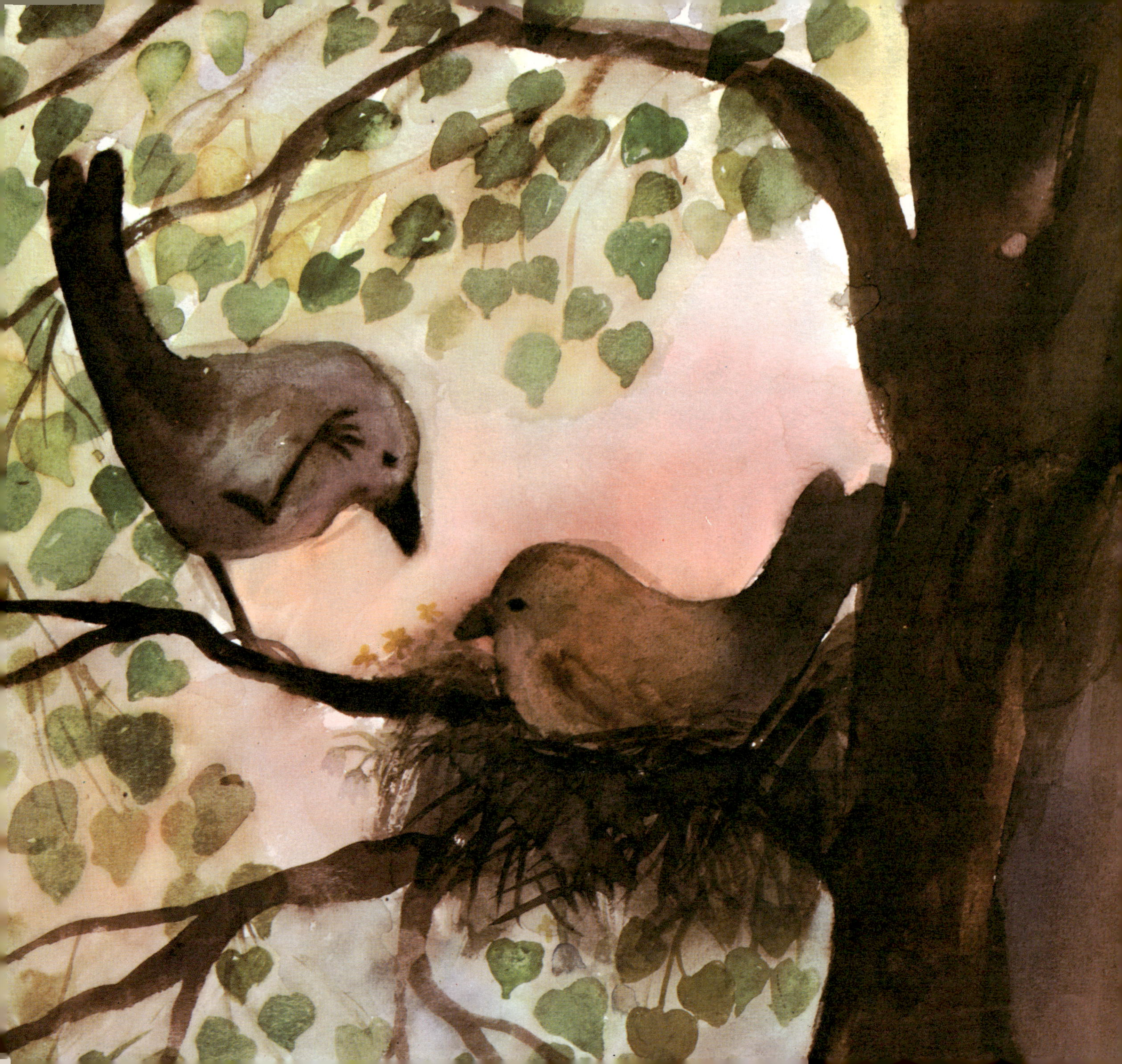

"But if we do that, O King —" said his men.

But King Vincent cut in:

"Do as I told you. My say is said."

Lord Tom-Tit swung up-side-down in the weeds as King Vincent said all this. He flew back to his nest. He put up his foot to scratch his sad little head.

Lady Tom-Tit sat on the eggs in the nest, soft and snug in her brown feather shawl.

"Why do you frown so, my pet?" she said. "Why do you put up your foot to scratch your sad little head?"

Lord Tom-Tit told her all that King Vincent had just said.

"He will snatch the bread out of our bills," he said. "And he will snatch it out of *his* bill, too. *We* keep his rye free from green-fly. But it is the weeds at the side of the rye-patch that keep it free from rust."

"But did not his men tell him so?" said Lady Tom-Tit.

"They did try to tell him," said Lord Tom-Tit. "But he shut them up with a brisk, *My say is said*. I see I must jog him and jolt him with the gift of a bit of my mind."

"How will you do that?" said Lady Tom-Tit.

And Lord Tom-Tit stood up tall, and told her:

"I will go to war with him."

He put on a belt of grass. From his belt he hung a long thorn. He put a nut-shell on his head as a helmet; and he took a nut-shell as a drum. He slung his drum with grass from his plump neck.

He had a twig for a drum-stick. He held his drum-stick with his wing.

He blew Lady Tom-Tit a kiss as she sat on her eggs. And off he went, *hop, hop,* to King Vincent's men. His drum swung to and fro on his plump chest. *Bang, bang,* went his drum-stick on his drum.

"Why do you bang a drum at us, Lord Tom-Tit?" said King Vincent's men.

And Lord Tom-Tit told them:

"To go to war with the king."

"Then we will bring you to him," they said.

And they led him in, to King Vincent.

King Vincent took him up in his hand.

"So you wish to go to war with me, Lord Tom-Tit?" said King Vincent. "But I hold you in my hand. What if I cut off your rash little head?"

"Do not do that, King Vincent," said Lord Tom-Tit. "And do not cut off the rash little heads of the weeds at the side of your rye-patch. If you do, you will get rust on your rye, and your rye will die."

"Is this so?" said King Vincent to his men.

"It is, O King," they said. "That is why weeds have stood at the side of the rye-patch so long that no-one can say *how* long."

Then King Vincent said to Lord Tom-Tit:

"Let us end this war, Lord Tom-Tit. I will not cut off the rash little heads of the weeds at the side of the rye-patch. You shall be lord of them."

Lord Tom-Tit took his nut-shell helmet off his rash little head.

The wind blew his hair into his eyes; but what of that?

He said, with a bob and a bow:

"My thanks to you, King Vincent."

And off he flew to his nest.

Lady Tom-Tit still sat on her eggs, soft and snug in her brown feather shawl.

"Did you jog and jolt King Vincent, my pet?" she said. "Did you win the war?"

"I did, and I did," Lord Tom-Tit told her. "I shook my drumstick at him. I said, *I hold you in my hand.* I said, *What if I cut off your rash big head?* I said, *I must be lord of the weeds at the side of the rye-patch.* I said, *My say is said,* I said."

"Did you say all that, my pet?" said Lady Tom-Tit. "Do get that drum and that belt off, and sit on that twig and sing me a little song. One chick will soon crack his shell. What shall we call him?"

"Let us call him Vincent, after the king," said Lord Tom-Tit. And so they did.

DO NOT GO INTO THE WOOD

A lark was born on open land, in a nest under a rock.

As he grew up, his mother said to him:

"Do not go far to hunt, dear. Stay in your own land. Stay in this open land, and find your food among its rocks."

"Why, Mother?" said the little lark.

And his mother told him:

"In your own land, dear, no hawk can catch you. But in a wood, no lark is a match for a hawk. So do not go into the wood."

For a time, the little lark was a good little lark, and did as his mother had told him.

Then one day he said:

"I *must* go and hunt in the wood!"

So off he went, to hunt in the wood.

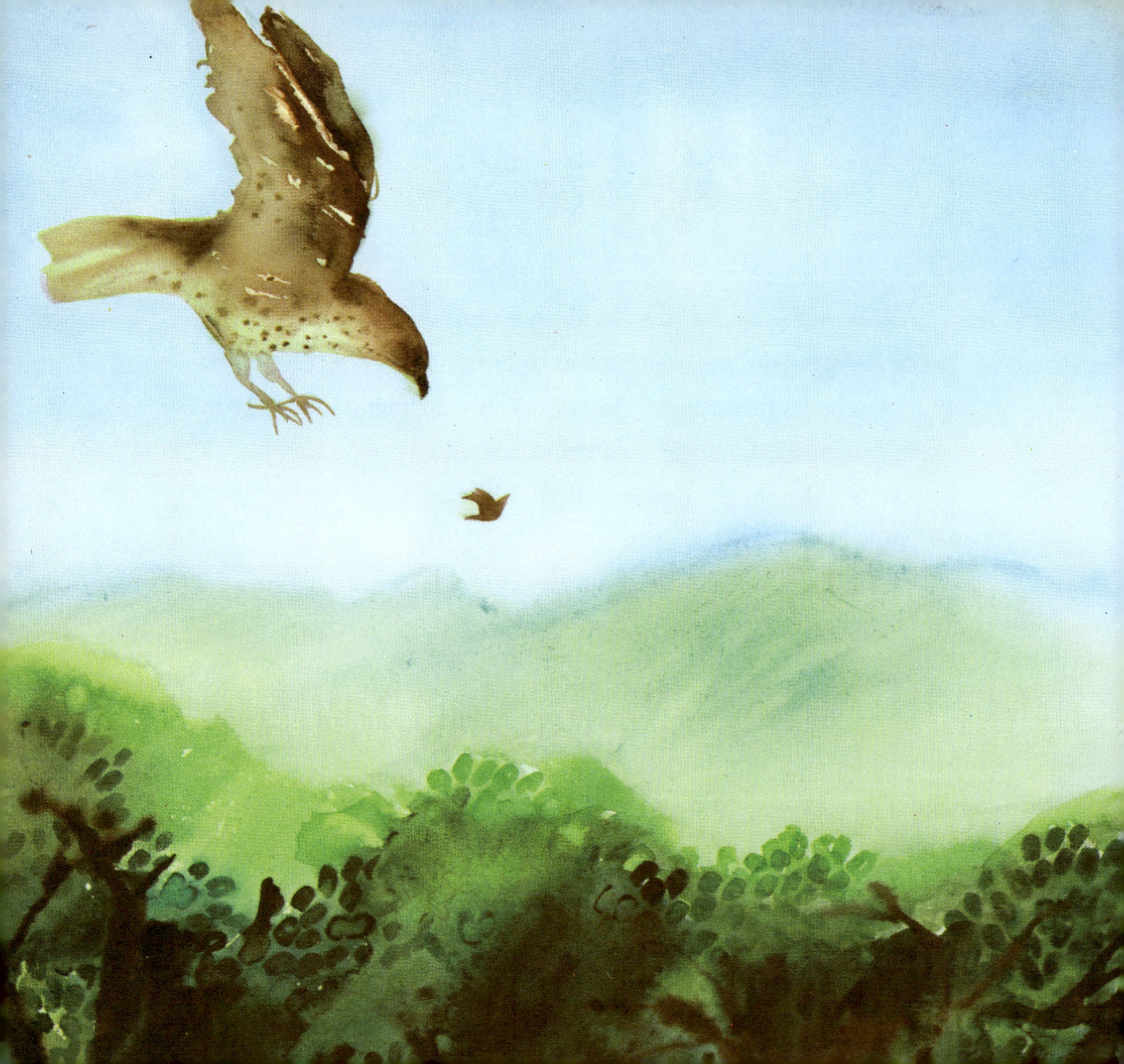

In the wood, a hawk saw him. He fell on him with a thud. In a flash, he had him fast in his sharp claws.

Then the little lark wept out loud:

"Oh, why did I not do as my mother told me?"

The hawk said to him:

"What did your mother tell you to do, my little lark?"

"To stay and hunt in my own land, and not to go into the wood," wept the little lark.

"And what land is your own land, my little lark?" said the hawk.

"The open land, among the rocks," wept the little lark.

"Why did she tell you to stay in your own land, my little lark?" said the hawk.

"In my own land no hawk can catch me," wept the little lark.

"Is that so?" said the hawk. "Let us go and try. But you will find I shall still catch you, my little lark."

So the hawk flew out of the wood, and into the open land, with the little lark still held fast in his sharp claws.

He put the little lark down on a rock.

The little lark stood still.

"Catch me, hawk!" he cried.

The hawk made his wings stiff. Flash, flash, he flew at the rock, to snatch up the little lark again in his sharp claws.

"Oh dear! The hawk is on me!" cried the little lark.

And with a little bob of his little head, he slid off the rock and down the rock and under the rock, all in one.

But the hawk hit the rock so hard that it made him puff.

"Well, well!" said the hawk. "To think such a little lark was a match for me!"

And from then on, the little lark did as his mother told him, and did not go again into the wood.

Two rhymes about spring-time and the cuckoo which are so old that the names of the writers are not known.

THE CUCKOO

The cuckoo's a bonny bird,
He sings as he flies;
He brings us good tidings;
He tells us no lies.

He drinks the cold water,
To keep his voice clear;
And he'll come again
In the spring of next year.

MAY DAY

Good morning, lords and ladies,
It is the first of May;
We hope you'll view our garland,
It is so sweet and gay.

The cuckoo sings in April,
The cuckoo sings in May,
The cuckoo sings in June,
In July she flies away.

The cuckoo drinks cold water
To make her sing so clear.
And then she sings Cuckoo: Cuckoo:
For three months in the year.

I love my little brother
And sister every day
But I seem to love them better
In the merry month of May.

THE CATERPILLAR

Brown and furry
Caterpillar in a hurry
Take your walk
To the shady leaf or stalk
Or what not,
Which may be the chosen spot.
No toad spy you,
Hovering bird of prey pass by you;
Spin and die,
To live again a butterfly.

Christina Rossetti

THE RAIN

I hear leaves drinking rain;
I hear rich leaves on top
Giving the poor beneath
Drop after drop;
'Tis a sweet noise to hear
These green leaves drinking near.

And when the Sun comes out,
After this rain shall stop,
A wondrous light will fill
Each dark, round drop;
I hope the Sun shines bright;
Twill be a lovely sight.

WILLIAM H. DAVIES

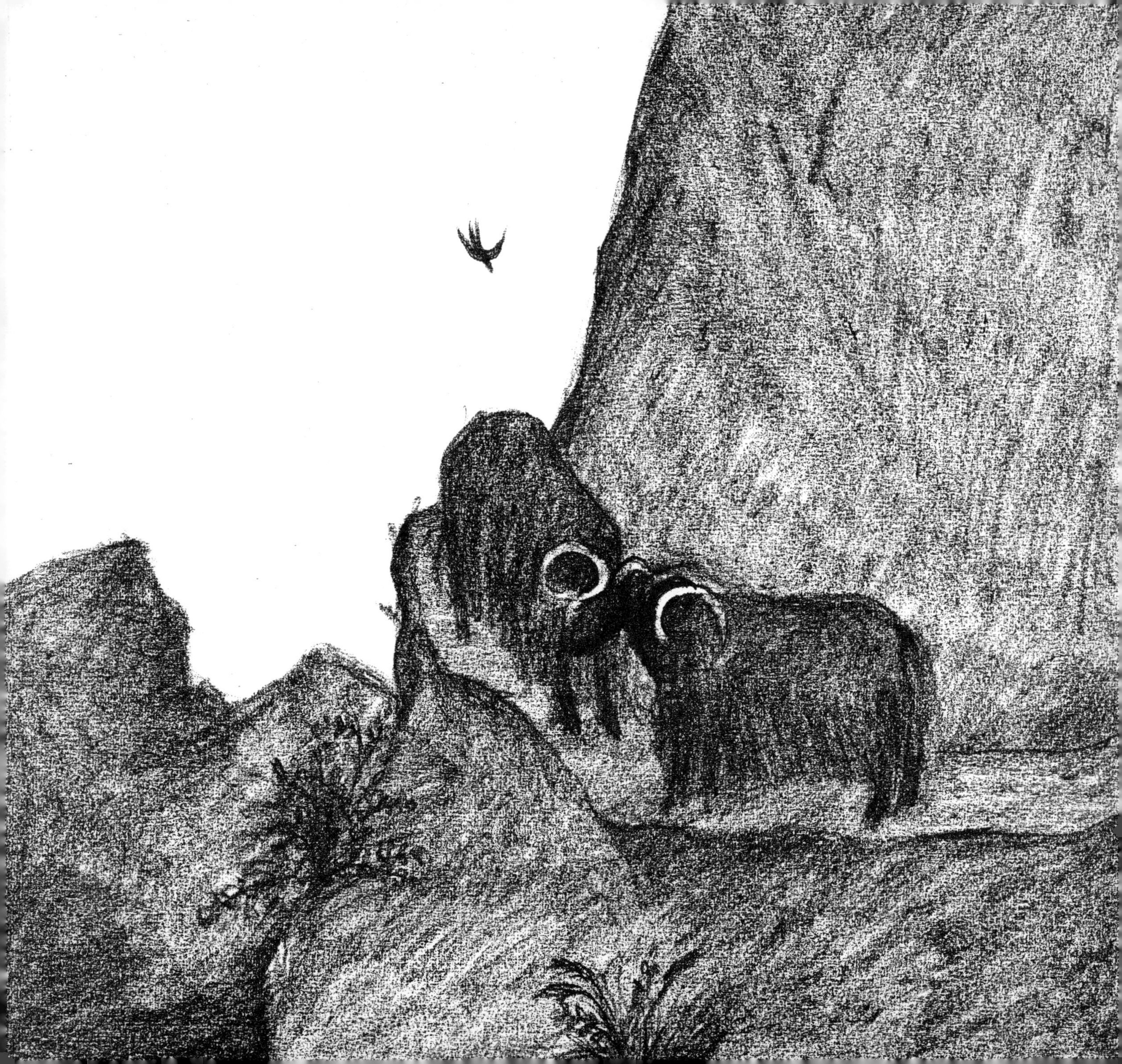

THE FORK-TAIL AND THE RAMS

Two rams met on a cliff-path.

"Let me go by," said Ram One.

"Let *me* go by," said Ram Two.

"It is for you to let *me* go by," said Ram One.

"No, it is for *you* to let *me* go by," said Ram Two.

"Get out of my way, you old ram!" said Ram One.

"Get out of *my* way, *you* old ram!" said Ram Two.

They both fell back, to get up speed. Then they ran, and met head-on, *crash, smash*.

"*Now* will you let me go by?" cried Ram One.

"Now will *you* let *me* go by?" cried Ram Two.

Again they both fell back, to get up speed. And again they ran, and met head-on, *crash, smash*.

A fork-tail saw all this as she sat on her eggs in her nest.

"I must stop them, or one of them will crack his skull," she said.

So she flew from her nest, to stop them.

She cried out to Ram One:

"Uncle, do not butt so!"

She cried to Ram Two:

"Uncle, be kind and stand still!"

But both rams still went on.

"What has it to do with you, Fork-Tail?" cried Ram One.

"Get out of the way, Fork-Tail!" cried Ram Two.

To and fro, *crash, smash,* went the rams. In and out, flip, flap, went the fork-tail.

Crash, smash, went the rams, just as she got in the way. When she flew free, she had lost the tip of her tail.

"If they *will* crack skulls, I must let them," she said. "For if it is *my* skull they crack, who will sit on my eggs?"

And hop, hop, hop, she went back to sit on her nest.

KING CACKLE

A king spoke so much that he got the nickname of King Cackle. A wise man said to him:

"Sire, all who talk too much talk some time at the wrong time. And much ill can come of that."

But the king made a jest of it.

"Next time you see ill come of it," he said, "tell me, Wise Sir."

Now a turtle had his lair in the mud in a pond in the hills. Two wild geese came to that pond.

They met the turtle as they swam on the pond. They grew fond of him.

The time came for the two wild geese to fly home. They said to the turtle:

"Friend Turtle, we wish we did not have to part from you. Why not come home with us?"

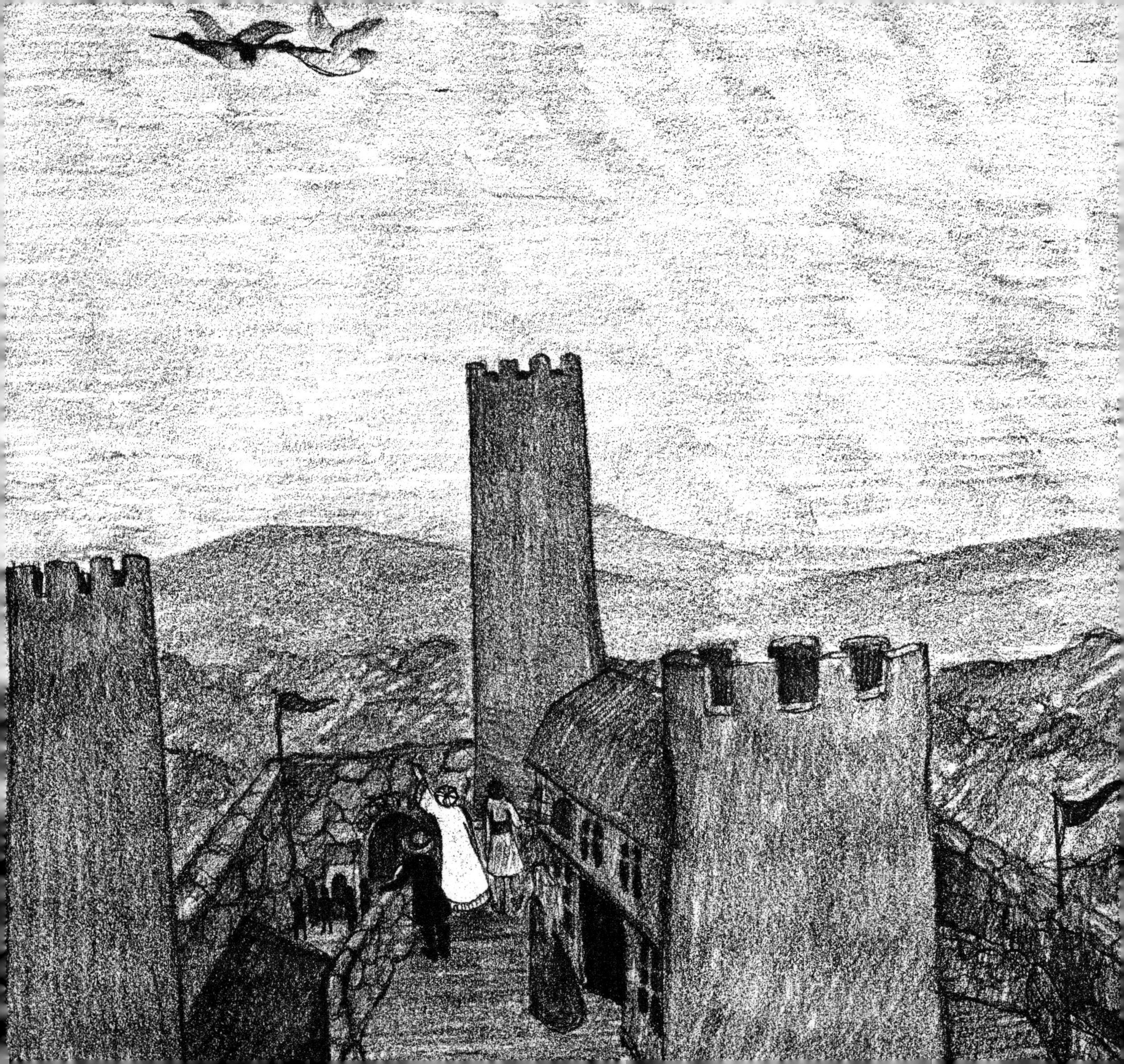

"How far is your home?" said the turtle.

And the wild geese told him:

"Only at the other end of the plain."

"That is too far for me," said the turtle. "My pace is so slow."

"Oh, you will not have to walk," said the two wild geese. "You can fly with us."

"But I have no wings," said the turtle.

"You will not need wings," said the two wild geese. "We will get a strong stick, and you can hang on to it by your teeth. And each of us will hold an end of the stick in our bills as we fly."

"Yes, I can do that," said the turtle.

So the two wild geese got a strong stick. Each of them held an end of the stick in his bill. The turtle held on to the stick with his teeth. And the two wild geese sprang into the air.

The wild geese flew fast. The wind went by with a swish. Soon they had left the hills, and now they flew over the plain.

In the plain stood the city of King Cackle.

In the city, men stood at the king's gate. They saw the wild geese pass over. They saw the turtle cling to the stick by his teeth.

"Look! Look!" cried the men. "A turtle in the air! I never saw a turtle fly till now!"

"And you never will again!" the turtle cried back at them.

As he spoke, he let go. Down, down, down he fell, to dash and crash and smash on the stone steps of the king's gate.

King Cackle went out to look at all that was left of the turtle. The wise man went with him.

King Cackle said to the wise man:

"Wise Sir, what made the turtle fall?"

"Sire," said the wise man, "you told me in jest to tell you next time I saw ill come of talk at the wrong time. This is that next time. The turtle spoke at the wrong time. So he came to this bad end."

"So the turtle, too, was a King Cackle?" said King Cackle. "I see I must mend my ways."

And he tried so hard to mend his ways that he lost his nickname. And in time he grew into a wise king, who spoke only at the right time.

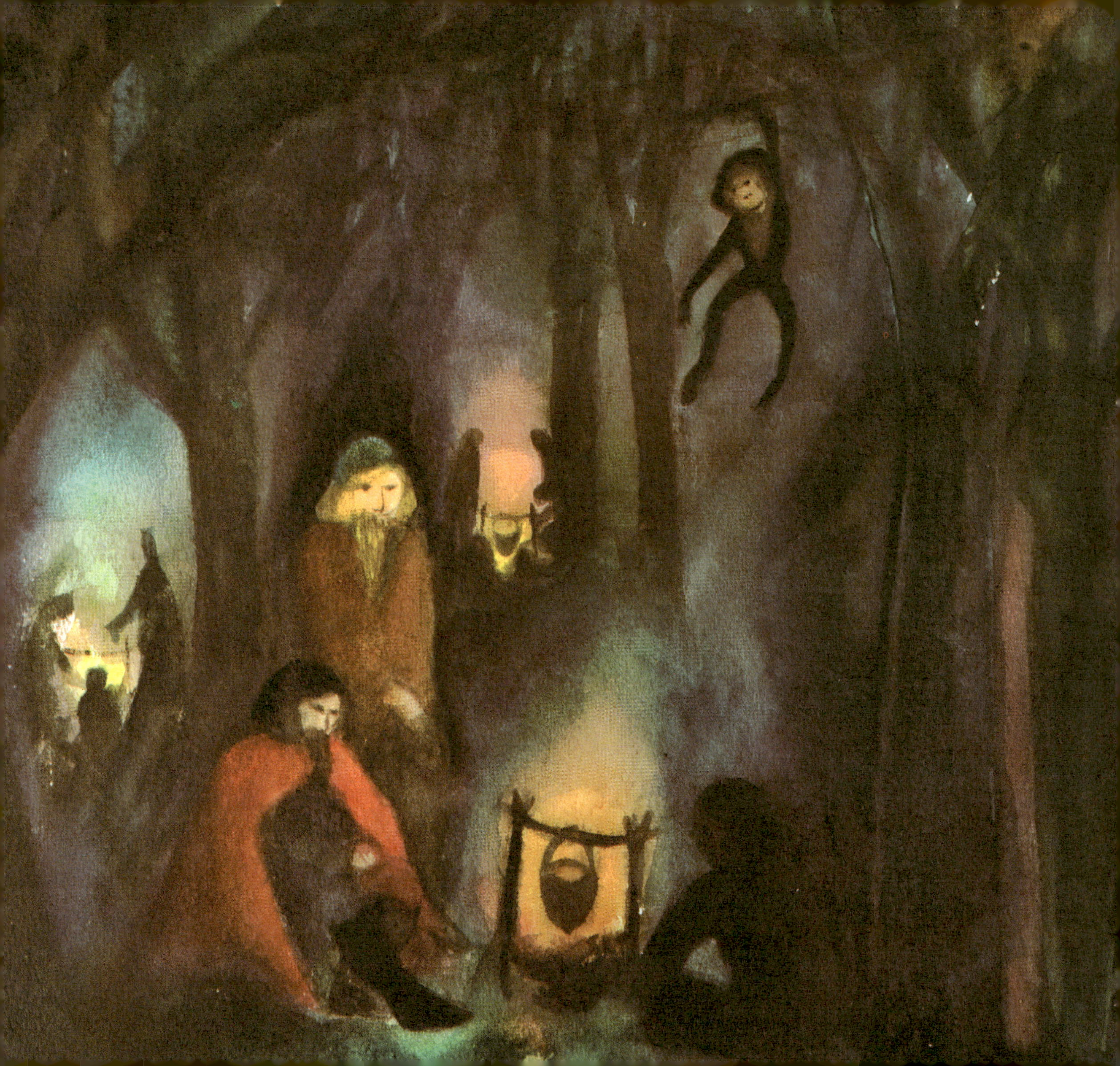

THE MONKEY AND THE PEA

A king was king of rich lands. Yet he made up his mind to go out with his men and win a poor one.

A wise man said to him:

"Sire, do not go. You have foes who will take your rich lands when you go to win this poor one. You will have lost much to get little."

"Still, I will go," said the king.

So he set out with all his men.

The wise man went with him, too.

At the end of the first day, the king's men made a camp among the trees. They lit fires, and set pots of water on them, to cook rice and peas to eat.

A monkey hung by one arm from a tree, to look with big eyes

at the peas.

Then he sprang down, to snatch at them. He got both hands full. Then he sprang back, and sat down in the tree, to eat them.

As he ate, a pea fell out of one of his hands.

So he flung away all the peas he held in both hands; and down he sprang from the tree, to hunt for his lost pea.

To and fro, to and fro he went. His little hands slid under each grass and twig.

But he did not find his lost pea.

At last he went back to his tree. Now he had no peas at all.

He sat glum and still, with a look of woe on his face.

The king had seen all this.

So now he said to the wise man:

"Wise Sir, what did you think of that?"

And the wise man told him:

> "Sire, I have seen this twice today.
>
> A king who casts rich lands away

To win a poor one, is not he

　　　Just like this monkey with his pea?"

The king stood still, to think.

Then he said:

"Yes, Wise Sir. So I am."

And back he went, with all his men, to keep his rich lands safe.

OLD RIDDLES

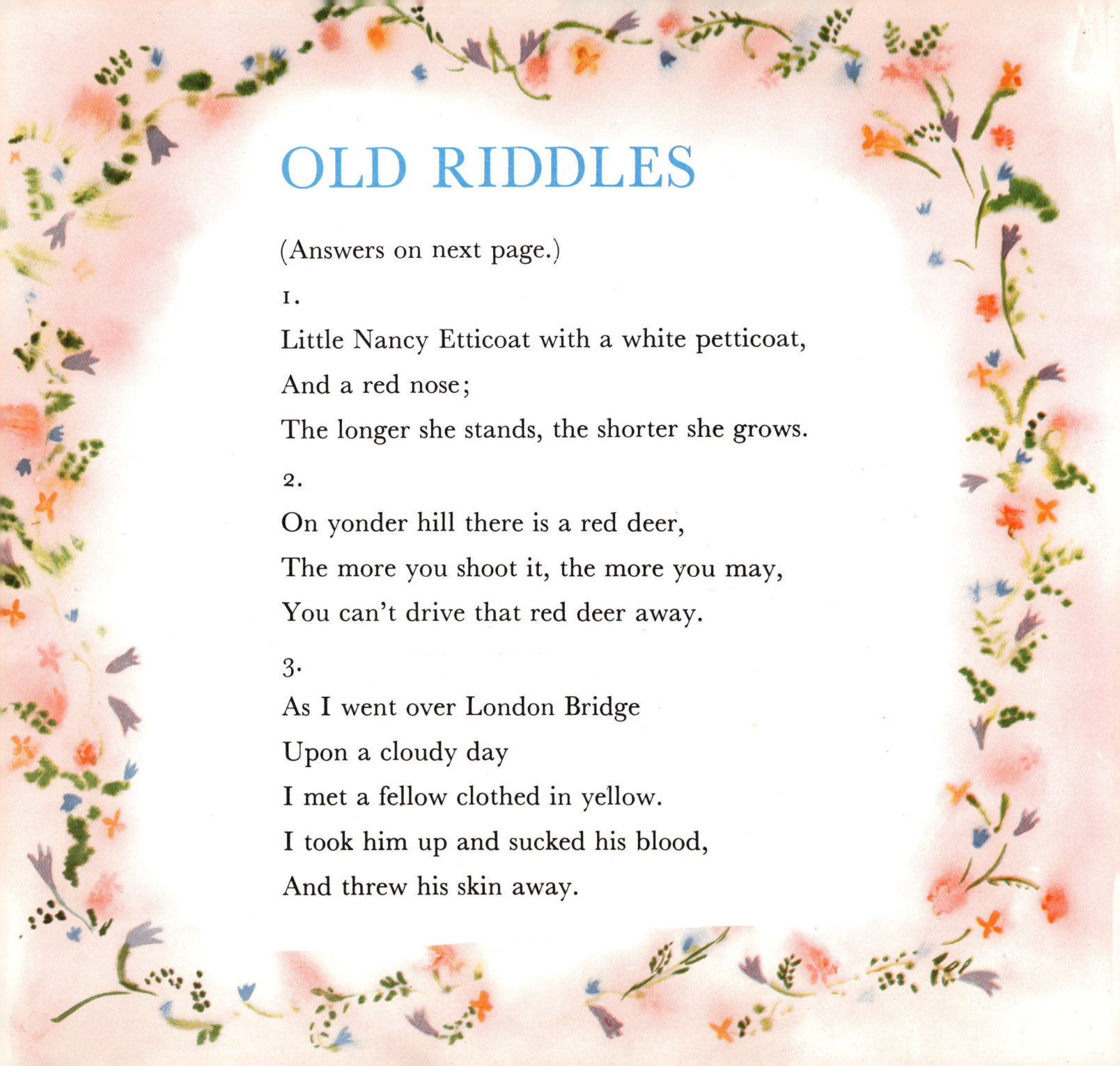

(Answers on next page.)

1.

Little Nancy Etticoat with a white petticoat,

And a red nose;

The longer she stands, the shorter she grows.

2.

On yonder hill there is a red deer,

The more you shoot it, the more you may,

You can't drive that red deer away.

3.

As I went over London Bridge

Upon a cloudy day

I met a fellow clothed in yellow.

I took him up and sucked his blood,

And threw his skin away.

4.
In marble halls as white as milk,
Lined with a skin as soft as silk,
Within a fountain crystal-clear,
A golden apple doth appear.
No doors there are to this stronghold,
Yet thieves break in and steal the gold.

5.
White bird featherless
Flew from Paradise,
Pitched on the castle wall;
Along came Lord Landless,
Took it up handless
And rode away horseless
To the king's white hall.

Answers to the riddles.

1. A candle.
2. The rising sun.
3. A blood-orange.
4. An egg.
5. Snow and the sun.

ABOUT THIS BOOK

This is the first of a series of reading-books intended for use in the Waldorf schools based on the educational principles of Rudolf Steiner. Both in the subject-matter and in reading standards these books will have as their foundation the general Waldorf curriculum, and, like the Waldorf education itself, one of their aims will be to awaken in the child joy and enthusiasm in acquiring new knowledge.

The first book can be used if desired at the end of the first year, and throughout the second year. The stories range in style and content from the fairy-tale element of Class I to the legends and animal-fables introduced in Class II. While rhythmical repetition of words and sounds, so necessary to children in the early stages of reading, is present to some extent in all the stories, it becomes less pronounced towards the end of the book, by which time a fairly wide and lively vocabulary will have been acquired.

A few poems have been included to satisfy the child's natural feeling for rhythm and rhyme, and thanks are due to the following for permission to use them:–

"THE RAIN". W. H. Davies. Copyright by Jonathan Cape Limited. Reprinted from THE COMPLETE POEMS OF W. H. DAVIES by permission of Jonathan Cape Limited and Wesleyan University Press, publishers; "THE HARE". Rose Fyleman. Permission to include the poem given by The Society of Authors as the literary representative of the estate of the late Rose Fyleman; "SOME ONE". Walter de la Mare. Permission to include the poem has been granted by the Literary Trustees of Walter de la Mare and The Society of Authors as their representative.

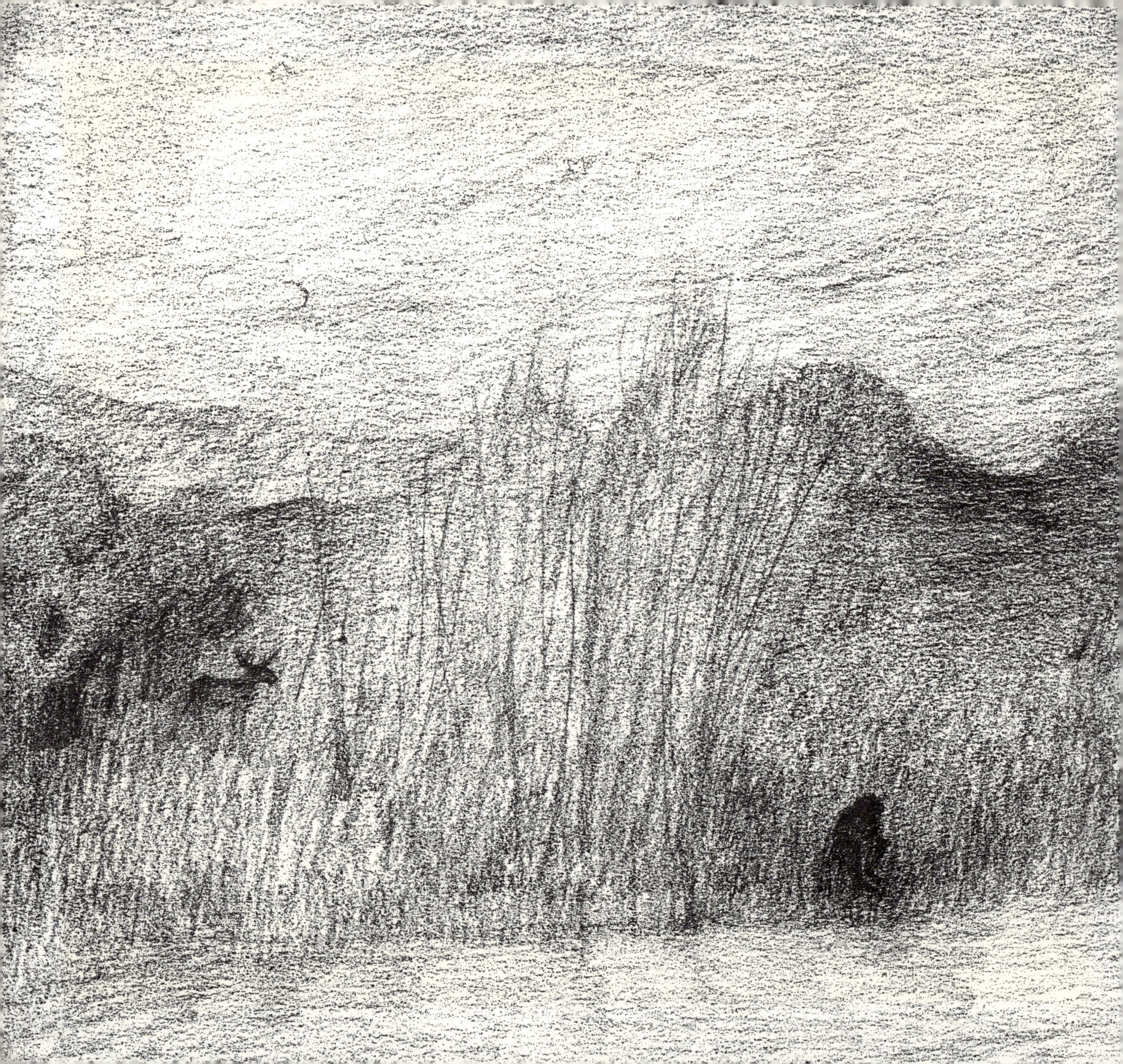